Joe Burrow: The Inspiring Story of One of Football's Rising Star Quarterbacks

An Unauthorized Biography

By: Clayton Geoffreys

Visit my website at www.claytongeoffreys.com
Cover photo by All-Pro Reels is licensed under CC BY-SA 2.0 / modified from original

Table of Contents

Foreword

Often times, when an NFL franchise selects a quarterback with its first-round pick, it ushers in a new era for that franchise. That was very much the case in 2020 when the Cincinnati Bengals selected Joe Burrow with the first overall pick of the draft. Burrow is one of the latest phenom passers to enter the National Football League. In college, he began as a backup at Ohio State, before transferring to LSU where he became the starter and leader of the 2019 Championship team. During that championship season, Burrow set records and won several awards such as the Heisman Trophy and Maxwell Award. It'll be exciting to see where Joe's career continues to go in the years to come. Thank you for purchasing *Joe Burrow: The Inspiring Story of One of Football's Rising Star Quarterbacks*. In this unauthorized biography, we will learn Joe Burrow's incredible life story and impact on the game of football. Hope you enjoy and if you do, please do not forget to leave a review!

Also, check out my website at claytongeoffreys.com to join my exclusive list where I let you know about my latest books. To thank you for your purchase, you can go to my site to download a free copy of *33 Life Lessons: Success Principles, Career Advice & Habits of Successful People.* In the book, you'll learn from some of the greatest thought leaders of different industries on what it takes to become successful and how to live a great life.

Cheers,

Clayton Geoffreys

Visit me at www.claytongeoffreys.com

Introduction

"It's the greatest story in college football." [iv]

- Kirk Herbstreit, ESPN, 2019

On December 19, 2019, Joe Burrow's name was announced as the Heisman Trophy Award winner, an honor that goes to the most outstanding college football player of the season. Before his speech, not many people knew a lot about Burrow other than the fact he had perhaps the most incredible college season of any quarterback in history and was on his way to leading the LSU Tigers to a perfect season and national championship.

But it was Burrow's speech that was as inspirational as any from an athlete accepting an award. People who did not know him were opened up to him and found him to be one of the most humble, most respectable, and most gracious athletes of all time.

And, as his statistics showed, one of the best as well.

Burrow struck a chord with millions of Americans as he stood in front of the microphone. It was perhaps some 30 seconds before he spoke his first word, overcome by emotion and wiping tears from his eyes. Most Heisman speeches are rehearsed, with notes so athletes can remember who to thank and what to say. But Burrow spoke straight from the heart—no notes, no prepared speech, no teleprompter. He was as real as anyone could be and his emotion could be felt in the room and all across the world.

Burrow struggled through those first couple of minutes, fighting back tears as he thanked his coaches, his players, and his family for making him the person he was and graciously acknowledging them for all that they did. After that, he went straight to the young generation of America. He reached out to *you*. There are kids out there who have dreams and aspirations of being great one day but are living in poverty or difficult circumstances. They struggle to put food on their plate and maybe never see their parents. Burrow immediately connected with those kids as he continued to fight back tears.

"Coming from southeast Ohio," Burrow said early in his speech, "it's a very impoverished area. The poverty rate is almost two times the national average. There are so many people there that don't have a lot. I'm up here for all those kids in Athens and Athens County that go home—not a lot of food on the table, hungry after school. You guys can be up here, too."[i]

Burrow continued to choke up and was incredibly emotional as he continued his speech. He was forced to pause at times and compose himself as the applause was heard. But while the applause on television was heard just in that room, it was resonating across all of America. "I'm just a kid that came down here from Ohio chasing a dream, and the entire state (of Louisiana) has welcomed me into their home."[ii]

It made all those kids out there who did not think they had a chance to make it like Joe Burrow a sense of hope. Burrow showed true leadership in his play and showed even more in the way he connected with his audience, in particular, those young kids in the Buckeye State of Ohio. Everything about that moment was so real. Even those that did not know who Burrow was before that speech felt a connection to him at that moment, felt the emotion, and looked up to him.

Letters written to Burrow came flooding in after his speech. This one was particularly special:

"Thank you for showing me and other children that no matter where you're from or your life story, if you work hard you can achieve greatness," the letter said. *"Also, thank you for giving back to your community. You have inspired me to not be embarrassed by my life story and work hard to achieve my goals. Again, thank you very much."*[i]

More letters just like that came pouring in. Will Drabold, who graduated from the same high school as Burrow, Athens High School, and also graduated from the University of Ohio where Burrow's father coached, was in awe and motivated by what he had heard. He immediately went on Facebook and started a fundraising page for the Athens County Food Pantry, which is supported by volunteers. He set the goal at $1,000, hoping to get some other people motivated by Burrow's speech just like he was. He posted that if anyone was motivated by the speech and would like to give money towards helping feed families in Athens, Ohio, to donate money.

Within an hour, Drabold had surpassed his goal. He had to immediately update the goal to $50,000 to accommodate the overwhelming response. Within 24 hours, Drabold raised over $80,000. Within a week, his fundraiser had surpassed $400,000. Within the month, it totaled over a half-million. Meanwhile, the Athens County Food Pantry's yearly budget was barely $80,000. They traditionally serve around 430 families and 1,200 people annually.[i] Needless to say, the remarkable outpouring of support motivated by Burrow's words was life-changing for the town.

Within a week, a wall on the Athens High School campus was painted with a picture of Joe Burrow and the words, "Congrats Joe Burrow. Thank You for Feeding Your Roots."[i]

This is just one of so many stories about how one athlete touched so many people in an encouraging way. Young athletes everywhere all have role models but there may be no one better to look up to than Joe Burrow.

Burrow is a true Cinderella story. Despite having achieved great success in high school, he was never a quarterback that college scouts were really passionate about. His dream was to play for Nebraska, the same school his father had played for, but they never gave him the time of day. However, he was recruited by Urban Meyer and given the opportunity to play for Ohio State, just 75 miles from where he grew up.

But shortly into his college football career, he was thinking of what his life would be like after school; the NFL seemed like a pipe dream at that point. He was redshirted and played sparingly in Columbus, backing up J.T. Barrett and Dwayne Haskins. And then, to make matters even worse, when he thought he might finally get a chance to compete for the starting job, he broke his thumb during camp.

As Ohio State began grooming other quarterbacks, even eventually landing Georgia's Justin Fields, Burrow decided to enter the transfer portal. That was when LSU and Coach Ed Orgeron took a chance on him.

"Coach O, you have no idea what you mean to my family," Burrow said in his speech after thanking Louisiana for taking him in. "I didn't play for three years; you took a chance on me not knowing if I could play or not. And I am forever grateful for you. Can you imagine a guy like Coach O giving me the keys to his football program? He just means so much to me and my family and to LSU. I sure hope they give him a lifetime contract; he deserves it."[ii]

It was at LSU under Orgeron that Burrow began to transform into the athlete that he aspired to be. It was not that he was not good at Ohio State, but with stacked talent at quarterback and a system that did not support his game like LSU's, If he had stayed at Ohio State, he likely would have graduated as a backup behind Justin Fields. Going to LSU gave him the chance to be a star, and was he ever! His numbers in 2019 were nothing short of incredible.

After ending the 2018 season by winning Most Valuable Player in the Fiesta Bowl in which he threw four touchdowns in a win against UCF, he went into the 2019 season with some confidence. He led all of FBS football with 5,671 yards and 60 touchdown passes. His 76.3 percentage completion was also the best in college football. Oh, yeah, and he also ran for

368 yards and 5 touchdowns, showing he could do it with his legs, too. He finished with a school-high and football-leading 202.0 rating.[iii]

Behind Burrow, LSU finished a perfect 15-0, beating Alabama in the regular season, and then crushing Oklahoma in the semifinal and Clemson in the National Championship game. To no surprise, Burrow was named the Championship MVP to go alongside his collage of trophies and awards that he collected in 2019. Along with the Heisman Trophy, Burrow was named the winner of the Manning Award, the Maxwell Award, the Davey O'Brien Award, the Lombardi Award, the Walter Camp Award, and the Johnny Unitas Golden Arm Award.[iii]

And there is more. Besides winning the National Championship MVP in 2019, Burrow also won the SEC Championship Game MVP, the Peach Bowl MVP, and was SEC First-Team and Player of the Year. Just a few months after winning the Tigers the national title, he was a no-brainer to be selected as the top pick in the 2020 NFL Draft. The Cincinnati Bengals brought Burrow home to Ohio, selecting him first overall and making him their future franchise quarterback.

Burrow had a solid opening season for the Bengals, throwing for 2,688 yards and 13 touchdowns in 10 games. However, he suffered a gruesome leg injury against the Washington Football Team and his season ended with a torn ACL. It was still a solid rookie season despite the lack of talent around him and the Bengals are looking to grow with him in the years to come.

Burrow's story goes back to his family who pushed him to always be the best. His father, Jim, also had a great college football career, playing linebacker for Tom Osborne and Nebraska. He eventually went on to be drafted by the Green Bay Packers, where he did not play much, and then had a career in the Canadian

Football League. After that, he then went on to coach at the collegiate level under Frank Solich at Ohio University.

Under the guidance of his dad and with a competitive push from his brothers, Burrow became a star athlete in high school. He led Athens High to a 37-4 record in the three years that he started for them and nearly won a state championship his final year there. In his final season at Athens, he threw an incredible 63 touchdowns and only 2 interceptions, earning him the honor of "Mr. Football" in Ohio, a title that goes to the best player in that state for that year.[v]

Burrow has gained the reputation of being one of the hardest workers in the sport, rising from what some might call "an average Joe" to a college superstar and NFL professional. With the help of Coach Orgeron, he became the quarterback that everyone dreamed of having in the 2020 NFL Draft.

"He (Burrow) means the world to me," Orgeron said. "He's one of the greatest players in LSU history. He's done so much for the state of Louisiana and LSU. We are so grateful for Joe Burrow."[vi]

Burrow's NFL career is just starting, but he has already done so much for so many people and inspired millions who already want to be just like the Bengals quarterback. It is incredible to think that there are so many more positive things to come from this young man. There are very few "Joe Burrows" out there, and before his NFL career ends, he could become one of the greatest role models and icons for the new generation of America.

Chapter 1: Early Childhood

Joe "The Athlete"

Joseph Lee Burrow was born on December 10, 1996, in Ames, Iowa to James and Robin Burrow. He has two older brothers, Dan and Jamie, whom he grew up with and has been close to his entire life.

When Joe was born, his father was coaching football at Ames High School. Jim Burrow would go on to be an assistant coach at Iowa State and the head coach for the Arena League team, the Iowa Barnstormers, during his time in Iowa. But Joe does not remember much of his early days in the Midwest.

"He doesn't remember anything about Ames; only what we've told him," said Jim Burrow. "He went to Ames High School games when he was just a few days old when I was coaching. But ultimately, what he knows is what he's been told. He was pretty young back then."[vii]

When Joe was eight years old, Jim was offered a Defensive coordinator position under Frank Solich at Ohio University and the family subsequently relocated to Athens, Ohio. He would remain coaching there until 2018 when Joe transferred to LSU.

Joe had a couple of favorite teams growing up. In college, it was Nebraska, where his father played football and where he had dreams of playing when he was older. The team lived briefly in Nebraska when Jim worked there during the 2001 season as a graduate assistant. But initially, when they moved to Ohio, Joe chose to root for the Browns over the Bengals. However, he quickly moved on and become a Saints fan because of Drew Brees, who ultimately became Joe's childhood idol. He admitted he followed the team intently and rooted for them during the years following Hurricane Katrina and when Brees and Reggie Bush became a force in the offense.

"I think he's (Brees) the best at what he does," Burrow said when he had the chance to meet Brees for the first time, which was just prior to winning the national championship. "That was my idol growing up. When I first met him, I was trying to be all cool, like, 'Yeah I know what I'm talking about,' but then on the inside, it's like, 'I'm talking to Drew Brees about football,' so it was really, really cool."[vii]

Burrow admitted in a laughing manner that he was a bit of a "bandwagon" fan growing up. After suffering for a couple of seasons with the Browns, he moved on and found himself rooting for the Saints.

But while Burrow loved football, it was basketball that Burrow thought he would likely excel at after college. He grew up in Ohio, where Lebron James was a star and who Burrow said was his favorite athlete growing up.

Burrow said he felt the pressure growing up to become a great athlete because it was a big part of his family's culture. Not only was his dad a starter for the Nebraska Cornhuskers and a college football coach, but Joe's paternal grandfather played basketball at Mississippi State; his uncle, John Burrow, played football at Ole Miss, and one of Joe's grandmothers was also a standout basketball player who once set a Mississippi state high school record when she accumulated 82 points in a game.[viii] And, of course, his older brothers were becoming star athletes, too. Both Jamie and Dan Burrow were elite high school football players and went on to play at the University of Nebraska, only increasing the pressure on Joe.

Joe was actually great in both football and basketball growing up. His father obviously wanted him to follow in his footsteps and become a great football player at Nebraska, but was open to him playing basketball, especially since he was so good at it. Prior to entering high school, Burrow shined as a guard in basketball and a quarterback in football in youth leagues. He entered with plans to play both sports—and potentially even baseball, which he also enjoyed.

The advantage that Joe had, though, was that he had a father who had been there at the top level in football, making it to the NFL for a brief time. Jim was able to pass the knowledge down to his son, and that meant a lot. He could coach him up in football based upon his own experiences, whereas he could not really do that in basketball. He helped develop him into a great young quarterback who was destined for success in high school. But, at the time, Joe's best talents still seemed to lie with basketball.

"He was playing middle school basketball and I remember telling his dad that I think something great is gonna happen with this guy," Jeff Skinner said, who was Joe's high school basketball coach. "This kid has that "it" factor. And that was before he even played for me."[ix]

Skinner said that Joe had a gift in basketball early on. He made the game look so easy. He would make passes you would never see anyone make. He was also a great leader on the court. Others looked up to him and followed his lead. Skinner knew immediately this was an elite athlete in the making.

Joe was always extremely competitive. Some called him "the quiet assassin". He may not have been the most boisterous player, but put any game in front of him, and he would want to beat you. And if he did not beat you, he would take it hard. He always competed in games against his older brothers, but because they were older than him and just as competitive and athletic, it was tough to beat them. But, rather than discouraging him, it only made him better.

Joe's parents also taught him the importance of education. Sports were always second; education was number one. They motivated him to excel in school. After all, you cannot play sports if you do not get good grades. Joe got good grades and then some. He was a smart student, getting nothing but As and Bs.

"He is naturally very smart," Adam Luehrman said, who became close friends with Joe when he moved to Ohio in 2005. "He has a very good memory. He was always one of the smartest kids in class."[ix]

While Burrow excelled at basketball and football, Luehrman was a great baseball player and played with Joe on the baseball team. But Joe's passion for baseball was not up to the same level as it was in football or basketball. Still, he was really good at it and if he had put the time into it, he could have gone places with it. However, Joe's motivation was deeper in the other two sports.

Adam Luehrman also played football with Joe and became one of his top wide receivers growing up, along with his twin brother Ryan. When they played in high school, Adam and Ryan were Athens High

School's top wide receivers, putting up near-record numbers with Joe Burrow as the quarterback.

"I wish I knew then I'd be catching passes from a future Heisman winner in high school," Adam said. "It was great being a receiver for him. Every throw was incredible. The confidence he showed at LSU, he showed in high school the same way. He pretty much led by example. You could tell the way he carries himself, he's very confident. He doesn't talk much but he's got a unique sense of humor."[ix]

Leadership was also something that Jim taught Joe, and because he had been a quarterback growing up, it was even more important to him. Jim taught his son how to treat players and coaches and take charge.

Joe was a bit different in that most leaders are talkative guys but Joe was quiet growing up, according to his childhood friends. He was very laid back, enjoyed playing video games, watching movies, and hanging out with his friends. But his friends always said that, while he was quiet, you could see the leader in him. Whenever things got rough, he stayed calm and helped give advice on how to handle certain situations.

"He was always a guy who just wanted to hang out," Adam said. "Even when he became famous, he didn't like the spotlight. He just wanted to talk with his friends and eat. He was so real. There was nothing ever fake about him."[ix]

Those are the best kinds of leaders and athletes to look up to. It is always heartwarming to hear that someone is not fake, that what you see is what you get. It is a treasure. So many times we look at an athlete and wonder if they are that way off camera as opposed to on. Every person you talk to about Joe Burrow has said that he is always the same person, whether a phone or camera is on him or not. The Joe Burrow that grew up as a teenager in Athens, Ohio has not changed a bit over time, even with the fame.

As Adam likes to say, "Everything may be different, but Joe is still Joe."[ix]

Joe "The Person"

While sports were such a huge part of Joe's life growing up, so was school. As already documented, Joe was a great student, getting As and Bs. But he was not just good with grades. He was good with his behavior. Teachers never had a problem with him and saw greatness in him from the beginning.

"It was a lot of fun being Joe's teacher," Chad Springer said, who taught Joe at Athens High School. "He was just amazing. The whole class was unique. They were eclectic. They did everything together no matter who they were, what sport they played. Extremely brilliant, intelligent, and a lot of fun to have."[ix]

Springer, along with many others that knew him, always laughed about his obsession with *Star Wars*. Whenever an assignment was made and you got to choose a theme, he seemed to always choose *Star Wars*. He even had a *Star Wars*-themed bedroom at his parents' place.

"I saw him as a great athlete and a great scholar," Springer said. "To see him go this far... I still picture him in my class at that front table with his friends playing on LEGOS building their project that had a *Star Wars* theme to this day.

"There were things about him you would want in any kid. Not just that leadership quality but he would walk some of our students with disabilities to class, make them feel a part of the group. Or, if you've got a kid who's kind of on their own, he would pick them to be on his basketball team. That's the kind of kid he is."[ix]

Hearing it come from his own teachers is such a telling sign of who he was as a child. No one ever said a bad thing about him. He connected with everyone. He was never a bully. He worked hard to make others feel like they belonged. He worked with students with disabilities, putting a smile on their faces. He helped those who were struggling in classes, tutoring them so they could improve their educational standing. There was not a student out there who was not accepted by Joe.

Stories like this are rare today, especially the way schools are. There are so many negative things being reported in the media, with bullying such a big part of our world. To hear how a young kid like Joe Burrow went above and beyond to help others and make them feel happy about themselves is inspirational and defines what a true role model is. Teachers and friends of his were not at all surprised when they heard his Heisman Trophy speech because that is who Joe Burrow is—always thinking of others.

"It was surreal," Springer said of Burrow's Heisman speech. "You watch a student, a person, who achieved something almost unfathomable to everybody. I've taught a lot of athletes who played for D1 schools, and this is above and beyond even that. You never think you're gonna see somebody achieve that great dream like that. He never thought he was better than anyone else and when he achieved this great success, it was almost as if you know the whole community was able to succeed because of him." [ix]

Burrow's teachers describe him as "the perfect role model." Someone who relishes where he came from when most people from Athens, Ohio are embarrassed by it. He wants people to never forget where they came from and appreciate it. Learn things from it and always look at the positive things in life. When there is a negative, do something about it.

"At one point his family thought about moving and he convinced them not to," Springer said. "He wants it known this is where he came from. In this community, it's very relevant for us to use him as an example of a success story. And it is a dream achievable. You can have dreams and achieve big things no matter who you are."[ix]

Joe was always committed to others growing up. He would take part in a lot of volunteer work and would do what he could to help around the house, according to his mother. He always kept the focus on the important things in life. When it was time for sports, that was his focus. When it was time to learn, he put all his emphasis on that. When he had free time, he devoted it to his friends or helping make the community a better place.

"If you had to do it all over again, in high school that's where he'd go again," his father said. "And to see where what led. The decision could not have turned out better for him."[ix]

Chapter 2: High School Career

Basketball Career

Going into high school, many thought it would be basketball that would be Joe Burrow's main sport, one that would carry him into college as he played for a premier Division I school. He himself even thought that it would be basketball where he would be looking for scholarships.

It was simply because of how good he was.

"He was a very, very tough basketball player," his friend Adam Luehrman said. "He was our point guard, shooting guard, he was the best 3-point shooter on the team, he was always the strongest guy on the team. He averaged the most points in our senior year. He was just as competitive in basketball as he was in football."[ix]

What made Burrow unique is that he could play multiple positions. While he was a guard on the roster, you could plug him anywhere and he could do it. He could rebound under the basket, he could create pick plays for other guys, he could block shots from the other team's tallest player, and he could shoot from anywhere on the floor.

"He was the ultimate chess piece. He was unlimited at what he could do offensively because we could move him all over the floor," head coach Jeff Skinner said. "We'd played him in the post a lot. And he would also guard either the quickest guy or, if the best player on the other team was a post player, we would have him guard him. If you can think of anybody versatile that could do anything, it was Joe."[ix]

Burrow was so good at basketball, he started on the Athens Bulldogs varsity team as a freshman, something he was not able to accomplish in football. That year, he helped lead the team to the Division II Sectional Championship and immediately garnered attention from college scouts.

According to Skinner, the other players could not believe he was a freshman. He just kept his head down, stayed quiet, but worked his tail off and it won over the rest of the team. Seniors looked up to how hard he worked. Sometimes the best way to lead is by example and Joe was doing that. He was never into trash talk, never into goofing off. He had a unique sense of humor but only used it when appropriate. When it came time to get to work and play, he was the best at it and players followed his lead.

"As we got into the season, the older kids liked him so much and he was so easy to get along with and so smart and such a good teammate, you would have never guessed by the time we were halfway through his freshman season that he was a freshman," Skinner admitted.[xi]

How often do you see that? Juniors and seniors looking up to freshmen? Usually, it is the other way around. Freshmen are usually intimidated by the older kids. Burrow flipped the script and had the utmost respect from the older kids on the team. Everyone bought into him and his play was only a small piece of it. It was all the other parts about him that people liked.

What made the transition from middle school to high school so easy for Joe was the Luehrmans. Ryan Luehrman also made the team as a freshman and Adam was there starting as a sophomore. There was a comfort in having guys he had played with his whole life around him.[xi]

Burrow's high school basketball resume was extremely impressive. He scored 1,426 points over four seasons, the second-most in program history. In his final season, he averaged 20 points per game and won Division II Southeast Player of the Year along with Michael Hall from Warren High School. He also had more than six rebounds per game during his career, so he was not just all offense. He also made First Team All-Ohio.

What was more impressive was how he continually got better as football became a bigger part of his life. Skinner respected the fact that Burrow was trending more in that direction, knowing that his quarterback skills were going to take him to the next level in that sport. He still got four years from Joe Burrow—and four years of *elite* play at that. He never let you down. He worked just as hard during his senior year as he did his freshman year and steadily got better.[xi]

Skinner recalled a time where Burrow had already signed on to play football for Ohio State and had to attend a camp the same day the team was playing a game in Indianapolis at the Hoosier gym. Skinner did not expect Burrow to attend the game, given that he had the football camp, but Burrow worked his butt off, finished his workout, drove 175 miles down to Indianapolis, and showed up on time for the Hoosier game ready to play. He was the very definition of dependable, coming through time and time again even when it was unexpected. He never put a coach, teacher, friend, or family member second in their life. This impressed Skinner as much as anything. He also had one of the best games of his season that day.

Colleges inquired about Burrow playing basketball and Skinner said he easily could have played Division I basketball if he had wanted to.

"I think he was definitely tracked toward a mid-major to high mid-major type of basketball player," Skinner said. "It would have taken the kind of focus and kind of work that he put in year-round for football to make that happen, but he was definitely on that track."[xi]

That mid-major school would have likely been Creighton, one of Burrow's favorite schools growing up. According to Jim Burrow, Creighton had shown high interest in Joe during his sophomore season and inquired about his desire to play college basketball. At the time, Joe was not sure which sport he wanted to pursue at the next level but took the Creighton interest seriously.[viii]

Burrow could have graduated early and foregone his senior year in basketball, transferring to Ohio State in the Spring so he could compete in camp and get a head-start on the upcoming season. Many top athletes do that, but Burrow did not want to do that to his basketball team or his friends. He wanted to be there for them during the season and celebrate graduation with his friends late in the spring. To him, that was more important.

"That's just how loyal he was to his friends and teammates and his team," Skinner said. "He meant everything to our basketball program. From an IQ standpoint to being this prophetic leader who did not have to say a word to lead, it was a thing of beauty to behold. Everybody just followed him."[xi]

Burrow's team, the Bulldogs, did not lose a single league game in his final two years and went 22-3 in his senior season. He was named the Tri-Valley Conference Ohio Division Most Valuable Player for his outstanding play his senior year. He was an All-State selection his final year and accumulated four All-Division honors. During his time there, the Bulldogs went on to win three sectional titles along with three league titles.[xi]

It is incredible to think that, as good of a player, role model, and leader that Joe Burrow was in basketball, he was even more elevated in football.

Football Career

By the time Burrow became the starting quarterback for the Athens Bulldogs in his sophomore season, he was an impressive 6'3" and 215 pounds. But he was not just the quarterback. Burrow was a two-way player and the team's best tackler and defensive player. If he did not go to college for his quarterbacking abilities, he could have probably made it as a cornerback or linebacker.

Burrow's defensive career started in the Division III State Playoffs against Tri-Valley. Athens was

36

undefeated but had to take on an offense that had a wing-T option and was difficult to contain. Defensive coordinator John Rogers recruited Burrow to play defense, knowing they needed a speedy presence and great tackler to contain the option. Burrow was phenomenal on both sides of the ball, scoring touchdowns and preventing touchdowns. A late interception by Burrow followed by a touchdown pass of his own helped cement a 41-20 win and advance the Bulldogs in the state playoffs.[xii]

But it was Burrow's quarterback play that was the real story of Athens High School. What made him such a great quarterback was his intelligence. Joe scored a 34 on his Wonderlic Test (which measures the person's cognitive abilities), which is higher than most quarterbacks in football. By comparison, Tom Brady scored a 33, Peyton Manning a 28, and Patrick Mahomes a 24.

In his first two starts as a varsity player, Burrow combined for 553 yards and 7 touchdowns. He helped lead the Bulldogs to the state playoffs in both his sophomore and junior year but failed to make it to the state championship. His senior year, however, was probably his best chance.

That year, the Bulldogs finished the regular season a perfect 10-0 and Burrow's stat line was, well, just ridiculous. Burrow threw for 4,445 yards and 68 touchdowns as opposed to just 2 interceptions! Thanks to Burrow, Athens scored an average of more than 60 points per game that season, including a game where they scored 82 and another where they piled up 77. In their first four playoff games, the Bulldogs won 65-14, 41-20, 52-20, and 34-31.[xiii]

Burrow led the team to their first-ever state championship appearance, a battle with Central Catholic High School. Burrow was unstoppable in that game. Not only did he rush for 59 yards, but he also threw for 452 yards and 6 touchdowns, including the apparent game-winning touchdown that gave the Bulldogs a 52-49 lead. But Central Catholic scored in the closing seconds to deny Burrow a state championship, beating the Bulldogs 56-52.[xiii]

According to MaxPreps, Joe Burrow threw for 11,416 yards in his three years as a starter, tossing 157 touchdowns and just 17 interceptions. That added up to 278.4 passing yards per game and a 68.6 completion percentage. Just as impressive were his rushing numbers. He kept the ball 370 times and ran for 2,067 yards, accumulating 50.4 yards per game.[xiii]

"We saw Joe do crazy things when he was here in high school," Athens offensive coordinator at the time, Nathan White, said. He took Athens High School—a school not notorious for its football program—all the way to the state championship. The thing I'm most proud about isn't his playing ability or the crazy stuff he's done on the field—it's how well he's handled everything and the leadership he displayed."[xiv]

Burrow had a career record of 37-4 as the Bulldogs starting quarterback and twice was named the Ohio Gatorade Player of the Year. He was also named Mr. Football USA in his senior season.

White described Burrow much like Skinner did. He was a true leader and always put others first. He was quiet but players followed him and looked up to him. He never took a play off. He gave more than 100 percent every time he stepped onto the practice or game field. He was a true competitor and an even better leader.

College Recruitment

Joe Burrow wanted to play college football. While he loved basketball and could have easily found a place on the starting roster for a Division I school, he relished the opportunity to play for a big school at the collegiate level.

His dream was Nebraska and his father did everything he could to try and pull strings for them to come to Ohio, watch him play, and offer him a scholarship. But, as good as Burrow's high school career started out, he was not getting the recognition or respect by scouts. In fact, the top recruits in the nation that get selected by colleges are four-star and five-star recruits. Burrow started out as a two-star recruit. That would rise as his high school career developed, moving up to a three-star after his junior season and then a four-star by the time he graduated high school. But by then, he was already off the board and had signed on with a school.

In 2014, Nebraska was coached by Bo Pelini, who would ultimately make the decision on whether to pursue Burrow or not. Joe's brother, Dan, played for Nebraska and badly wanted the Cornhuskers to recruit his brother. "All Joe ever wanted to do was play for Nebraska," Dan Burrow said. "It was his dream."[iv]

There were some doubts about Burrow from a lot of scouts that led to his rating being lower than his statistics showed in high school ... His arm strength was a question that many college coaches frowned upon. He was still ranked as one of the top 300 players in the 2015 recruiting class and listed as the No. 8 best dual-threat quarterback in high school football.

The 2014 season was when Burrow was deciding where to go to school. Nebraska saw his tape and he hoped to get an offer from them. But it was not long before Burrow heard back from the school and found out that his dream had been shot down.

"They told me I wasn't good enough," Burrow said.[iv]

It was a heartbreaking moment. The entire Burrow family was upset. Pelini would end up fired after the 2014 season and Mike Riley, who took over shortly after the 2014 season, said the team would not be recruiting a quarterback. Thus, Burrow would begin to look at other places.

While many schools passed on Burrow just like Nebraska did, there was one man from a big university who was enamored with him. Tom Herman, who was the offensive coordinator at Ohio State at the time (and would later become the head coach at Texas), visited Athens and watched Burrow work out. He could not believe what he saw.

"Yeah, that was probably the best I've ever thrown my entire life," Burrow said. "I walked off the field and said, 'If they don't offer me after that one, then I'm just not good enough.' But he kinda fell in love with me that day, went back to Columbus, and kinda stood on the table for me."[xv]

Some coaches and scouts from Ohio State were not so convinced about Burrow and did not think the team should pursue him, but Herman stood strong and persuaded head coach Urban Meyer to sign him. Meyer had a lot of faith in Herman and brought Burrow to Columbus where they would work him out and eventually offer him a scholarship to play for Ohio State.

Ironically, during the final meeting between Meyer, Herman, and the Burrow family, Herman had to step out to take a call. That call was from the University of Houston who had been talking with him about taking over their football program. Herman would agree to coach at Houston the same day Burrow signed on with the Buckeyes.

Burrow was excited to play for Coach Meyer and Ohio State but knew winning the starting job would not be easy. Burrow was told he would be redshirted his first year so he could gain more experience and would then compete for the starting job. Ohio State had just won a national championship and had high hopes with J.T. Barrett moving forward. Meyer was an excellent recruiter and got some of the best quarterbacks in the country to play for him, so Burrow had to be at the top of his game if he was to ever start for Ohio State.

Chapter 3: College Career

"Buckeye Backup"

When we think of Joe Burrow the college player, we think of him as LSU superstar, Heisman trophy winner, and national champion. But when he began his college career, LSU was honestly one of the last schools on his mind, and the Heisman Trophy was a distant dream. He was just hoping one day to start at quarterback for Ohio State, which was going to be difficult given the crop of quarterbacks the team had.

Urban Meyer had a knack for recruiting quarterback talent. After all, at Utah and Florida, he recruited and developed Alex Smith and Tim Tebow, two of the greatest college quarterbacks of all time. In 2014, Meyer even won a national championship with a third-string quarterback, Cardale Jones. Braxton Miller and J.T. Barrett were five-star recruits out of high school that Meyer had turned into gems but both got hurt towards the end of the 2014 season. Dwayne Haskins was another young recruit just entering college that Burrow would have to eventually beat out if he wanted to win the starting job. Haskins, though, would not come into the picture until after the 2016 season.

While Burrow had a great high school career, he was still a long way off from where he wanted to be. The truth is, many promising high school quarterbacks enter college as five-star quarterbacks but ultimately end up failing. It is not easy. You go up against much more challenging defenses than you did in high school and the environment is much different. You need to stay focused and not get too ahead of yourself. You might think you had worked really hard to get to that point—but at the college level, you soon realize that you have to put in 10 times the work you did previously to succeed. And that is on top of taking college classes, which are much more demanding than high school courses.

Burrow knew this, however, and knew that it was not going to be easy. Once having dreamed of going to Nebraska, he now used Nebraska's rejection as fuel to prove to them he was indeed worth signing. First, though, he would have to learn and develop. And In his redshirt year, he did just that, working practices and learning terminology, working hard to get better. He would go to games and watch on the sidelines as a redshirt player.

In 2015, it was Barrett and Jones who went back and forth at quarterback, with Barrett eventually landing the starting position. Barrett would be with the team until the 2017 season. Meanwhile, Burrow bided his time and focused on honing his skills and learning as much as he could. He had his eyes on 2018 as the year he would lead Ohio State.

Burrow played in five games during the 2016 season as he backed up J.T. Barrett. He saw his first appearance in the team's opening game against

Bowling Green. After Barrett compiled six touchdowns in the game and Ohio State took a huge lead, Meyer took out the starters and put in the backups, including Burrow. It was then that he threw his first college touchdown pass, a 36-yarder to Demario McCall on the way to a blowout 77-10 win.[iii]

It would be the theme of the 2016 season. Barrett was the starter, but when the team got up big, Burrow, the backup, would see playing time. Burrow went 22-for-28 for 226 yards that first season and 2 touchdowns. The Buckeyes made it to the College Football Playoffs but were crushed by Clemson 31-0 in the semifinal.[iii]

While Meyer never stated that Burrow was not developing the way they had hoped, they never committed to him being the starting quarterback after Barrett graduated. 2017 was Barrett's senior year, but the team had also recruited highly coveted quarterback Dwayne Haskins. Haskins would compete with Burrow for the backup quarterback spot in 2017 and the winner of that battle would start the 2018 year after Barrett left. Ohio State also recruited Tate Martell and he would also eventually be in the mix, but would not factor in.

Burrow won the backup job at camp and was listed on the depth chart as the backup to Barrett. Just like the season before, he saw limited action, throwing for 57 yards in 4 appearances. But during the season, Burrow broke his hand and Haskins moved up into the backup role, getting some of the playing time that Burrow would have gotten.

Then, in the team's finale against one of their fiercest rivals, the University of Michigan, Barrett suffered a knee injury that put him on the bench and Haskins replaced him. Haskins made the most of that opportunity—an opportunity that Burrow would have had if he had stayed healthy.

Haskins came in trailing 20-14 and helped rally the team, leading them to 17 unanswered points on the road at Ann Arbor to give Ohio State a huge 31-20 win over the Wolverines. Haskins impressed and won over the fans and many of the coaches with that performance. After all, if you are an Ohio State quarterback and help lead a rally to beat Michigan, you are going to be popular. Haskins had seen other playing time that year, playing eight games and finishing with 565 yards and 4 touchdowns while finishing with a rating of 173.1. But that win at Michigan meant a lot.[iii]

With Barrett graduating, it set up a huge spring camp quarterback battle between Haskins and Burrow. "It was an open competition, but we all basically know that Burrow was going to have to knock out the champ (Haskins)," Ohio State beat reporter Bill Rabinowitz said. "If you go into Ann Arbor and rally the Buckeyes to a win, that's a massive thing on your resume."[xix]

The competition was reported to be extremely heated between Burrow and Haskins and neither quarterback really won out. According to Rabinowitz, it was basically a dead heat, no one standing out over the other. But Burrow wanted confirmation he was going to be the starter. He did not want to spend his junior year on the bench. While he never said it publicly, he did not feel like he was going to win the job over Dwayne Haskins. And he was starting to see more backup reps in practice.[iv]

The competition would likely go into the fall and Burrow did not want to take that chance. He had worked hard in school and after his third season with Ohio State, fourth overall in school, he had graduated. Thus, he went to Urban Meyer and offensive coordinator Ryan Day and had a heart-to-heart. He asked if he could transfer. Meyer and Day both respected Burrow's wishes and allowed him to seek other options.

"There were no hard feelings," Rabinowitz said. "For Burrow, there was no reason to stay if he wasn't going to be the starter. He earned the right to explore his other options. Meyer and Day watched both of them play and wanted both to stay, but respected Burrow's wishes and thought he earned the right to move on. It was a completely understandable move by all sides. It was a win-win."[xix]

Down the road, it would indeed be a win-win. Haskins had an incredible 2018 season at Ohio State, helping lead them to a huge Rose Bowl victory. But surprisingly, he left early for the NFL Draft. The Buckeyes, however, were still able to get a superstar transfer in Justin Fields, who took Ohio State to the 2020 College Football Playoffs and helped them beat Clemson in the semifinal.

Burrow was grateful to Ohio State for giving him the opportunity. He never once said anything bad about the school. He understood the situation and how it had played out. It was time for him to find a new school and a new journey, a journey that would be better than he could have ever dreamed.

Becoming a Tiger

Again, Joe Burrow was looking for a place to play college football, and again, Nebraska was at the top of his list. It was a mulligan for the Cornhuskers, who had just hired Scott Frost to be their new head coach, the Nebraska alum who helped take UCF to a perfect and undefeated 2017 season.

Burrow would have loved to have gone to Nebraska but when Frost was confronted with the quarterback transfer, he said, "no thank you." They were content with what they had in quarterback Adrian Martinez. So, once again, Nebraska had a shot to land Joe Burrow and they turned him down. Just for the record, the 2019 and 2020 Nebraska Cornhuskers went 5-7 and 3-5 respectively and did not play in the postseason. The decision to shun Burrow left many Cornhuskers fans disgusted.

In the end, Burrow focused on two schools that had expressed the most interest: Cincinnati and LSU. Cincinnati had a major edge and was thought to be the school where Burrow would end up going. It was closer to home and their head coach, Luke Fickell, had coached as an assistant at Ohio State in 2015 and 2016 and knew Burrow very well. The week prior to transfer signing day, Burrow was heavily leaning towards becoming a Cincinnati Bearcat.

But Ed Orgeron, the head coach at LSU, set his sights on Burrow and would put on a strong campaign push to bring him to Baton Rouge. Orgeron had watched film of Burrow with his coaches when looking at potential transfers. When Orgeron watched Burrow on film, he was blown away and told his coaches that they needed to do whatever it took to bring him in. "This guy is a game-changer and difference-maker," he recalled saying. "All ball."[xx]

On the second weekend in May, Orgeron arranged to fly Burrow down with his dad and his brother Dan. He ordered crawfish and Cajun food to help reel in the Ohio quarterback and his family. Also in the meeting was offensive coordinator Steve Ensminger and defensive backs coach Bill Busch. Busch had spent time at Ohio State under Urban Meyer and knew Burrow. Orgeron would use him as a recruiting tool, and Busch would end up spending time with the Burrows over the weekend, taking them out to eat and discussing the LSU program.

Orgeron then ran through film with Burrow, showing him different plays and asking him how he would handle certain situations, almost like a test. Burrow passed it with flying colors and was impressed with Burrow's answers. "We had a nice cut-up of some of the plays that he ran and some of the plays we run. We asked him to take us through his reads. He was excellent," Orgeron said. "He knew exactly what was going on, exactly the coverage, the reads. We went

56

through some quarterback run plays. He was A-plus in that meeting."[xx]

Burrow came away impressed with LSU after that weekend but perhaps the final cherry on the sundae was Dan Burrow. Joe's brother Dan lived in Houston and, after a heart-to-heart talk, Joe convinced his brother to move to Baton Rouge. Orgeron later stated that all his family was on board with him moving to Louisiana instead of going to Cincinnati.[xx]

"As we leave, Coach O is like, 'Did you get my number?'" Dan Burrow said. "That was cool. We kept in touch throughout that next week. Joe really had to sit down and think about it. He told us he wants to play football at the highest level. 'If that's true,' I told him, 'there's LSU and there's Cincinnati. There's only one answer.'"[iv]

Another huge advantage was the opportunity to play in the SEC against some of the best teams in the country. While Orgeron never promised Burrow the starting job, given the lack of talent they had at the position at the time, it appeared that it would be Burrow's position to lose. He had an excellent chance of winning the job in camp.

After the weekend was over, Burrow had made up his mind and decided to move to Baton Rouge and play for "Coach O" at LSU. It was a huge victory for the Tigers, who badly needed a quarterback to take that next step. They already had outstanding prospects in wide receivers Justin Jefferson and Ja'Marr Chase and running backs Nick Brossette and Clyde Edwards-Helaire. Getting a strong quarterback to operate that offense could give the Tigers a chance at the national title in the near future.

Another selling point for Orgeron to pursue Burrow was Meyer himself. The legendary college coach put in a strong word for Burrow, gushing about his work ethic and how he has advanced as a quarterback over the years. He had noticeably improved a lot on his arm release and arm strength, two things that had held him back from becoming a five-star recruit.

Other players that knew Burrow from Ohio State also gushed about him, telling LSU they were getting a superstar quarterback and incredible leader.

"Believe me when I say this because he was my roommate for two years," Ohio State defensive lineman Dre'Mont Jones said. You're getting a dog in Joe. Joe's no slouch. He's a leader. He's gonna take over that huddle."[xxi]

"He's a determined hard worker, very smart. Just me knowing Joe, he's gonna do what it takes to win," said offensive lineman Isaiah Prince. "He's gonna make the necessary throws and the necessary reads. I know how Joe works and I think they're extremely blessed to have a player like Joe."[xxi]

To this day, there are no hard feelings between Burrow and Ohio State. Burrow was grateful to Urban Meyer and the coaching staff in Columbus for helping him to become a better quarterback and did not feel he would have had the success he went on to achieve at LSU if it were not for their efforts in developing him.

Junior Year (2018)

It did not take long for Joe Burrow to be announced as LSU's starting quarterback for the 2018 season. But there were still significant challenges for Burrow, as he would have to learn to manage the game through a run-first offense. In fact, through his first 10 games as a Tiger, Burrow threw just seven touchdowns, had zero 300-yard games, and just two 200+ yard games. By comparison, in his final 18 games, he threw 87 touchdowns and had 15 games where he threw over 300 yards. It was like two completely opposite careers at LSU.

LSU was leaning on running backs Nick Brossette and Clyde Edwards-Helaire early on in the season, both of whom had twice as many touchdowns as Burrow in those first 10 games. Burrow's best game would come against Ole Miss at home. After tossing just three touchdowns in his first four games, Burrow found the end zone four times against the Rebels. He threw for 292 yards and 3 scores while also running for 96 yards and a touchdown. He finished with a near-perfect rating of 209.7. Burrow displayed the dual-threat talent that LSU had invested in and showed what the future would be like in Baton Rouge.[iii]

While the second season saw Burrow finish every game with a rating easily over 100, sometimes 200, in his first nine games, he failed to eclipse it three times. One of his most difficult games came against the Florida Gators, a school always known for its defense. LSU had climbed to No. 5 in the rankings and traveled to No. 20 Florida. The Gators forced Burrow into two interceptions and he finished with just 192 passing yards as LSU lost their first game of the year, 27-19.[iii]

The other team that frustrated Burrow was the defending national champions, Alabama. Playing at home in primetime in front of a raucous, sold-out Death Valley Stadium, Burrow threw for just 184 yards and failed to throw a touchdown while getting picked off as the Tigers were decimated by the Crimson Tide in every facet of the game. Not only could Burrow get nothing going but neither could the running game. In the end, the Tigers failed to score a single point, the first time they had been shut out since they had lost to Alabama 21-0 in the 2011 National Championship Game. Alabama beat LSU 29-0.[iii]

Perhaps the wildest game of the year came in Burrow's final regular-season game that year. Playing Texas A&M, the two teams got into an overtime battle that seemed like it would never end. Burrow threw for three touchdowns and ran for three touchdowns in a marathon battle that went on for more than five hours. But LSU ended up on the losing end, 74-72, in *seven* overtimes![iii] (To this date, there have never been more than seven overtime periods in a college football game.)

In that game, Burrow was struggling to keep his legs up. Burrow had been beaten, battered, and bruised throughout the matchup. During halftime, he was getting IVs put in his arm and being given food to energize him. During the game, the trainer was constantly pumping fluids into him, trying to keep him in the game. Burrow, though, was a warrior and fought as hard as he could until that seventh overtime.

"To see somebody put that kind of effort, desire, and passion into a game," longtime head LSU trainer Jack Marucci said, "it's probably one of the first times I've seen anyone get into that kind of state of fatigue."[iv]

Burrow shrugged off the beating, saying that was what he loves most about football. "I enjoy getting hit sometimes," Burrow said. "It makes me feel like a real football player instead of a quarterback. People can look down on quarterbacks if they're not taking hits."[iv]

Despite three losses that year, LSU still got the opportunity to play in a New Year's Six Bowl close to home. The Fiesta Bowl selected No. 11 LSU and No. 7 UCF to square off in Arizona. It was seen as the game where Ed Orgeron finally let Joe Burrow loose. The Tigers were a more balanced team, but from the Fiesta Bowl until the end of 2019, they became a passing attack that seemingly no one could stop.

For most of the 2018 season, LSU had kept Burrow hidden a bit, his throwing abilities obscured by the team's run-first offense. Orgeron, though, felt like it was finally ready to unleash him. The true test would be in the Fiesta Bowl, a game where Coach O would ditch that run-first offense and let Burrow throw freely.

"For Joe, [the talent has] been there," running back Clyde Edwards-Helaire said. "It just wasn't displayed a lot because of the offense we were running."[iv]

Burrow and his receivers played catch with each other during the Fiesta Bowl and connected four times for touchdowns. These were not short touchdowns, either. Trailing 14-3, Burrow first connected with Justin

Jefferson from 22 yards out to cut the Knights lead to 14-10. Then, when Burrow got the ball back, he went right back to work. He hit Derrick Dillon deep on a 49-yard bomb to put the Tigers ahead. Just a few minutes later, Burrow connected with Jefferson a second time, this time from 33 yards out to extend the Tigers lead.[xxii]

On the opening drive of the third quarter, Burrow found Ja'Marr Chase from 32 yards out to give LSU a 31-21 lead. Burrow would then lead them on three more scoring drives that resulted in field goals and helped the Tigers beat the Knights 40-32. Burrow threw for 394 yards and 4 touchdowns, his best game yet as a Tiger. He was named Fiesta Bowl Most Valuable Player.[xxii]

"It looked like the passing game we wanted," Orgeron said. "Joe was on the money."[xxii]

It was a great way to go into the offseason. LSU had shown the potential they had and were returning most of their starters for 2019. Little did anyone know just how wildly successful they were about to become.

The Dream Season (2019)

In Joe Burrow's first five games of the 2019 season, he was doing things that no LSU quarterback before him had ever done. In those first five games, he threw for nearly 1,900 yards and 22 touchdown passes. He had over a 200 rating in four of his first five games.

In the team's opening game against Georgia Southern, traditionally known for their defense, Burrow was nearly flawless, completing 23 of 27 passes for 293 yards and 5 touchdowns while finishing with a 232.8 rating. The Tigers easily routed Georgia Southern 55-3 to start the season with a bang.[iii]

But it was the second game of the season that really caught the media's attention. Doing it against Georgia Southern was one thing, but doing it on the road, in primetime, and against a top-10 Texas team? Yes, that was on a totally different scale.

LSU came into the game ranked No. 6 facing off against the No. 9 Longhorns. Texas traditionally has great defensive backs, but not even they could contain Burrow and the LSU passing game, which positively torched the Longhorns defense. Justin Jefferson ran circles around the defense and Burrow found him time and time again. He hit Jefferson twice for touchdowns in the first half to give the Tigers a 20-7 lead halfway into the game.[iii]

Then, leading 37-31 late and backed up on their own 39, Burrow let one loose and found Jefferson once again down the field. The perfectly thrown ball landed right in Jefferson's hands and he took it in for his third touchdown of the game, giving LSU a commanding lead as the clock was rapidly disappearing. They would hold on for the 45-38 win.[iii]

It was a career game for Burrow, who threw for 471 yards and 4 touchdowns against Texas, finishing with a 209.8 rating. Burrow continued beating up on defenses in the next three games and helped get the Tigers off to a 5-0 start before a showdown at home against the No. 7 Florida Gators—the team who had shut Burrow down a year ago.

The Gators were one of the few teams in 2019 who went the distance with LSU, hanging in there with them the whole game. The two teams were tied 21-21 at halftime, with Burrow already having thrown two touchdowns.[xxiii] Trailing 28-21 in the third quarter, Clyde Edwards-Helaire, who ran for 134 yards, found the end zone to once again tie the game at 28. LSU then added another score late in the third quarter to go up by a score.[xxiii] Looking to land the knockout punch, Burrow maneuvered his team down the field in the fourth quarter before hitting Ja'Marr Chase on a perfectly thrown 54-yard touchdown pass to give LSU a 42-28 lead, a lead that would stand to give LSU a very satisfying 6-0 start to the season.

Burrow did not take any credit himself, instead giving it all to the guys who allowed him to throw for 301 yards that night.[xxiii]

"We know last year they got after us up front," Burrow said after the game. "Our offensive line took that personally. I'm so proud of those guys. There was no pressure the entire night."[xxiii]

In the next two games, LSU took care of business against Mississippi State and Auburn. Burrow threw for four touchdowns in a big win over Mississippi State but struggled against a strong Auburn defense who played toe-to-toe with LSU and managed to get to Burrow repeatedly. Still, Burrow threw a crucial touchdown in the second half to give LSU a 23-20 win, setting up a monster showdown with their arch-rival, Alabama, in primetime on the road.

LSU was No. 3 while Alabama was No. 2 going into the match, one that was perhaps the most anticipated of any game that college football season. A year ago,

Alabama had completely dominated the Tigers and Joe Burrow, winning 29-0 on their way to yet another College Football Playoff appearance.

But 2019 was different and Joe Burrow showed early just how much improved LSU was from a year ago. If Alabama had any vulnerability, it was their defense, and Burrow took full advantage from the very first drive. Six minutes into the game, Burrow hit Chase from 33 yards out to give LSU the lead—one that they kept the whole night.[xxiv]

In the second quarter, Burrow hit Terrace Marshall and Edwards-Helaire for touchdown passes to give the Tigers a commanding 33-13 lead at halftime. Alabama just had no answers and could not slow Burrow down. When they put more guys in the secondary, Edwards-Helaire destroyed them on the ground. Edwards-Helaire compiled four touchdowns in the game, three on the ground, as LSU shook off Alabama in the second half when they were closing in.[xxiv]

Leading 39-34 late, Burrow lead LSU on another scoring drive to nearly put the game away, 46-34. Alabama was not going down without a fight, however. The Crimson Tide next scored on an 85-yard touchdown pass from Tua Tagovalioa to Devonta Smith to cut the lead to 46-41, but their onside kick failed and LSU hung on for their biggest and most exhilarating win of the year. Burrow finished the game completing 31 of 39 passes for 393 yards and 3 touchdowns.[xxiv]

"He's (Burrow) one of the best we've ever had here," coach Orgeron said after the win. "But we've still got four games left and we're going down the road, we're going to try and win every game and we're going to bring a championship back to Louisiana."[xxiv]

"We're not done yet," Burrow added. "It's Game 9. We've got three more regular season-ones and the SEC Championship. This was never our goal. We've got bigger goals than this."[xxiv]

Orgeron and Burrow were true to their words. Joe stayed focused and continued to dominate defenses in the final three weeks of the regular season. LSU was dominant in wins against Ole Miss, Arkansas, and Texas A&M. He threw for 11 touchdowns in those 3 games and had over a 200 rating in each game. When the college football playoff poll came out, LSU was ranked No. 1 ahead of Clemson and Ohio State. Alabama, who had lost to Auburn in their last game of the regular season, was out of the playoff picture for the very first time in the playoff era.

The Tigers still had a daunting task ahead of them, however. In order to secure a spot in the playoffs and the top ranking, LSU would have to beat No. 4 Georgia in Atlanta in the SEC Championship, which was not an easy task. Georgia was led by a very talented Jake Fromm and had a dangerous running back in D'Andre Swift.

But, despite facing a mostly Georgia crowd, LSU dominated from the very start. Burrow threw two touchdown passes in the first quarter to give the Tigers an early 14-0 lead. Leading 20-3 in the third quarter, he tossed two more touchdowns to put the game out of Georgia's reach before the fourth quarter even arrived. The Tigers cruised to an easy SEC Championship victory, 37-10, over Georgia. Again, Burrow shined, throwing for 349 yards and 4 touchdowns in the game.[iii]

The win put LSU in the College Football Playoffs for the first time and also gave Joe Burrow the inside track to win the Heisman Trophy later that month. Burrow finished the season completing 402 passes for 5,671 yards, ranking No. 1 in FCS. He also led all of college football with 60 touchdown passes and a 76.3 completion percentage. His 202.0 rating ranked second only behind Tua Tagovailoa.[iii]

The Heisman Trophy

Joe Burrow, Jalen Hurts, and Chase Young were all invited to New York for the Heisman Trophy Presentation, but most everyone expected Burrow to take home the honor. He had already racked up a lot of accolades before that night. He was named the Maxwell Award winner for Best College Football Player and the Davey O'Brien and Manning Award winner for Best College Quarterback. He would also go on to win the Lombardi Award and Walter Camp Award and was First-Team All-SEC.[iii]

There was no drama when the final results were counted and Burrow's name was announced as the Heisman Trophy winner. He received 841 of the 891 first-place votes, one of the biggest landslide victories by a player in the award's history. In fact, only O.J. Simpson received more first-place votes when he won all the way back in 1968. Burrow broke the record based on points, securing 93.8% of points available, breaking Troy Smith's record in 2006. Oklahoma's

Jalen Hurts finished second, followed by Ohio State's Justin Fields and Chase Young.[xxv]

Burrow thanked everyone that had made winning the award possible, starting off with his offensive line, who he credited with giving him the time to make the plays necessary to win games and lead the offense. He went on to thank his coaches, his family, and everyone who played a role in him being there.

"I'm just so thankful for LSU and Ohio State," Burrow said. "Great coaches in both places. And all my teammates have welcomed me into the Bayou as brothers.

"I've tried to leave a legacy of hard work, preparation, loyalty, and dedication everywhere I go. I'm surrounded by such great people that make easy."[xxvi]

He was once called by some in the media "Average Joe". He was considered by Nebraska not good enough to play for them. Now he was the best college football had.

"This is what kids dream of doing," Burrow said. "I envisioned myself on that stage and being the quarterback of the No. 1 team in the country playing for the national championship. So this entire season has been a dream come true for me."[viii]

But as much as the Heisman Trophy meant to Joe Burrow, he wanted more. According to him, the only statistic that mattered was the 13 wins, which got them the chance to play for the national title. He wanted to finish the year Number One, ahead of Ohio State, Clemson, and Oklahoma, and holding up the championship trophy in New Orleans in a few weeks.

2019 Playoffs

Burrow faced a lot of pressure as he tried to accomplish both a Heisman Trophy and the National Championship in the same season. Some quarterbacks in the modern era have been able to achieve that feat, such as Cam Newton, Jameis Winston, Charlie Ward, and Danny Wuerffel, but others have failed to live up to the hype in the big game, such as Gino Torretta, Troy Smith, Eric Crouch, and Sam Bradford.

Burrow's road would first go through the Peach Bowl in Atlanta in the first national semifinal against the fourth-ranked Oklahoma Sooners and quarterback Jalen Hurts.

Oklahoma was dynamic on offense and had one of the top receiving weapons in the country in CeeDee Lamb. But defensively, could they contain Burrow?

That question was answered nearly immediately. From the first time Joe Burrow touched the ball, Oklahoma defenders were trying to catch LSU wide receivers to no avail. By the end of the first half, Burrow had shattered records and erased any doubts.

Less than three minutes into the game, Burrow went right down the field and connected with Justin Jefferson from 18 yards out to put LSU ahead early. After Oklahoma answered with a score, Burrow hit Terrace Marshall for a score to put LSU ahead 14-7.

Then, with just over a minute to go in the opening quarter, he again hit Jefferson for a touchdown, this time from 35 yards out.[xxvi]

The touchdowns kept coming. LSU got the ball right back and Burrow again let it loose. He went deep for Jefferson once again and tossed a perfect 42-yard pass for a touchdown to give LSU a 28-7 lead. It was touchdown number four for Burrow. Just three minutes later, Burrow again hit a couple of quick strikes before launching another perfect pass to Jefferson, this time from 30 yards out. Touchdown number five.[xxvi]

Leading 35-14 and still in the first half, Burrow next launched a bomb to Thaddeus Moss and put it right on the money, a 62-yard touchdown pass. Touchdown number six. And Joe still was not finished. LSU got the ball back right before halftime and Burrow went back to work. He connected over and over again before finding Marshall from two yards out to put LSU up 49-14. Touchdown number seven—and it *still* was not even halftime yet.[xxvi]

Those seven touchdowns tied a bowl game record and the seven touchdowns *in one half* broke an all-time record. He opened the second half with yet another drive down the field and this time took it in himself from two yards out for his eighth overall touchdown of the night to put the game completely out of reach, 56-14, allowing LSU to begin resting their starters in advance of the national championship game. By the end of the game, LSU had crushed Oklahoma 63-28 in the Peach Bowl.[xxvi]

It was no surprise that Burrow was named the game's Most Valuable Player. He was 29 for 39 for 493 yards and 7 touchdowns. He averaged 12.6 yards per completion. He also added 5 carries for 21 yards and a score. Justin Jefferson led all receivers with 14 catches for 227 yards and 4 touchdowns, proving to everyone just how good a wide receiver the NFL would be getting in 2020. His four scores tied a bowl record.[xxvi]

"We go into every game thinking no one can stop us," Burrow said.[xxvi]

"One team, one heartbeat," Orgeron added after the game.[xxvi]

LSU now had their eyes on the bigger prize: the national championship. To be the champs, they would have to *beat* the champs. In the second semifinal, the Fiesta Bowl, the defending national champions, the Clemson Tigers, edged out Ohio State to reach their fourth title game in five seasons.

Clemson was led by a superstar quarterback of their own, Trevor Lawrence, also destined for NFL success with the Jacksonville Jaguars. Lawrence was 25-0 as the Clemson Tigers starting quarterback. They had a more physical defense than anything LSU had faced all year and also had some intimidating weapons surrounding Lawrence, such as Travis Etienne and Tee Higgins.

LSU entered the game as a six-point favorite as people touted their offense as maybe the greatest of all time. However, could they beat the experienced Clemson Tigers, a team that has "been there and done that" so many times before?

It was one of the most hyped national title games of all time because of the matchup: Lawrence vs. Burrow. Swinney vs. Orgeron. Edwards-Helaire vs. Etienne. Tee Higgins vs. Justin Jefferson. Tigers vs. Tigers.

LSU had a huge edge, though: The 2019 National Championship Game was being held at the New Orleans Superdome, less than 60 miles from Baton Rouge. That resulted in LSU being able to have more of a home crowd feel for the game, and Burrow would later go on to say it played a huge role.

The first half of the national championship proved every bit as good as advertised as the two teams traded blows. Clemson got off to a fast start when Lawrence led his team down the field and ran it in from one yard out to give Clemson an early 7-0 lead. Clemson's defense had kept Burrow in check early, but finally, Burrow broke out. With just two minutes left in the opening quarter, Burrow hooked up on a team pass with Ja'Marr Chase from 52 yards out, tying the game at 7.[xxvii]

But, in the second quarter, it began to look like Clemson was taking command of the game. They answered with 10 unanswered points to go up 17-7 midway through the second quarter. That was when everything changed. Burrow would battle back with three unanswered scores. First, in less than a minute, he zipped right down the field and took it in himself from inside the five to cut the lead to 17-14. Just four minutes later, he connected with Chase a second time for a touchdown to give LSU the lead. Then, with just 10 seconds left before halftime, he hit Moss from six yards out to give LSU a 28-17 halftime lead.[xxvii]

Burrow and LSU proved in the second half of the second quarter just how scary their offense was. Clemson's defense, touted as one of college football's best, was completely bewildered by Burrow, who scored three times. Every time it seemed like Clemson would have an answer, LSU bounced back. In the third quarter, when Clemson was able to cut the lead to 28-25, Burrow bounced right back, leading his team down the field and connecting with Moss again for a touchdown to give LSU a 10-point lead, 35-25.[xxvii]

When Clemson failed to answer, Burrow knew another touchdown could put the game away. He orchestrated a drive down the field and had Clemson on their heels. Then, from the 24-yard line, he threw a perfect pass to Marshall for a touchdown, giving LSU an insurmountable 42-25 lead. Clemson knew they were finished. The rest of the game played itself out and LSU were national champions, beating Clemson 42-25.[xxvii]

Burrow would go on to win the Most Valuable Player Award for the National Championship, throwing 5 touchdown passes and 463 yards. He also displayed his dual-threat ability, running for 58 yards and a score. Edwards-Helaire also ran for 100 yards and Ja'Marr Chase capped off a spectacular career night with 221 yards receiving.[xxvii]

"He's one of the greatest players in LSU history," Orgeron said of Burrow after the game. "He's done so much for the state of Louisiana and LSU. We are so grateful for Joe Burrow."[xxvii]

For Joe, it was an incredible journey to get to this point. Just two years ago, he was in a battle just to try and be a starting quarterback in college football. A lot of teams did not want him, including Nebraska. But Burrow got the last laugh and stood atop all of football.

"This is what I wanted to do from the time I was five years old, was hoist this trophy," Burrow said after the game. "And bringing it back to Louisiana, I guess we're in Louisiana, but staying in Louisiana, we weren't going to let someone come in here and steal this from us in our home state. We have a great fan base that came out and supported us. We were going to keep this thing right here."[xxvii]

Burrow's college career ended in dream fashion. He was now looking forward to the NFL and was undoubtedly already being targeted by the Cincinnati Bengals, who held the No. 1 overall pick in the 2020 NFL Draft.

Chapter 4: NFL Career

The Draft

The 2020 offseason was one of the strangest, if not *the* strangest in history, because of the COVID-19 pandemic. But since the virus did not overcome the nation until March and April, prospects were able to showcase their talents at the NFL Combine and in Pro Days, which were held prior to those months.

Burrow, however, did not compete in the NFL combine; rather, he attended, took his measurements, and did interviews. He worked out on Pro Days and was pretty much a lock to be drafted by the Cincinnati Bengals with the first overall pick.

Because of the COVID-19 pandemic, the Draft was done virtually. NFL Commissioner Roger Goodell announced the draft picks in a room and cameras were inside the homes of players, coaches, and general managers. When the Bengals were put on the clock with the first overall pick, they immediately let the commissioner know their pick: Quarterback Joe Burrow from LSU.

"It's a dream come true," Burrow said. "To get to play so close to home, me and my family couldn't be more excited about it."[xxviii]

Some thought Burrow should have refused to go to what many deemed to be a terrible team like Cincinnati. In the past, some players had announced that they refused to play for a certain team because they had no direction. For example, Bo Jackson told the Buccaneers not to draft him first in 1984. They did and Jackson subsequently boycotted the NFL and went straight for baseball until the Bucs gave up his rights. Eli Manning refused to play for the Chargers when they drafted him and ultimately was traded to the Giants.

Burrow was not like that, though. He would play for anyone. That is who he was. The Bengals were certainly a really poor team with lots of holes, but that excited Burrow. He took it as a challenge and was enthusiastic to be the centerpiece of a new direction.

"I feel the best attribute I can bring to the Bengals is leadership," Burrow said. "I feel I've always been good at bringing everyone together to form a common goal, and I think my work ethic kind of permeates throughout the team."[xxviii]

The Bengals needed a leader and Burrow was the perfect fit for that franchise. By also drafting wide receiver Tee Higgins of Clemson, the Bengals gave Burrow a big and fast body to throw to.

Burrow was anxious to get to work and win the starting job. At first, it looked as though he might start the season on the bench, but once the Bengals traded Andy Dalton to the Cowboys, the Cincinnati Bengals were firmly committed to Joe Burrow starting Week 1.

2020 Season

Joe Burrow would start his NFL career against the Los Angeles Chargers, a team that had also drafted a rookie quarterback in the first round, Justin Herbert. However, Herbert started the opening game on the bench. It was not long after an injury to Tyrod Taylor, however, that Herbert found himself facing off with Burrow.

Burrow's opening game was one you would expect from a rookie. It had its fair share of ups and downs.

Burrow showed a lot of promise and hope but also missed some throws, including throwing an interception. He was 23-for-36 against the Chargers for 193 yards. The highlight of the game came late in the first quarter where Burrow escaped traffic and darted up the middle of the field for a 23-yard touchdown run, his first score as a pro.[xxix]

However, leading 13-6 going into the fourth quarter, the Bengals defense could not contain the Chargers. Joshua Kelley ran in from five yards out to tie the game and Michael Badgley kicked the game-winning field goal to give the Chargers a 16-13 victory in Burrow's first professional game.[xxix]

"I made too many mistakes," Burrow said. "I missed A.J. (Green) on a deep ball, I missed John on a deep ball, I threw the interception. That just can't happen."[xxx]

Burrow's second game showed a lot of promise. In a Thursday Night showdown in Cleveland against the

Browns, Burrow proved why the Bengals selected him first overall. Burrow and Baker Mayfield got into a shootout, and Burrow threw his first touchdown as an NFL player. Before the game was over, he would throw three of them. He connected on 37 of 61 passes for 316 yards and 3 scores, but again, the defense just could not stop the opposing team in critical moments. The Browns beat the Bengals 35-30.[xxix]

The 61 passes were the second-most pass attempts all-time by a rookie quarterback. Burrow also became the first rookie since 1950 to throw 60 or more pass attempts in a game and not throw an interception.[xxix]

In 10 games that season, Burrow had 300-plus yards in half of them. He also had four multiple-score games. It was not bad for a team that really was struggling on the offensive line and lacking the weapons that most other teams had. Following the loss to the Browns, Burrow threw for 312 yards and 2 scores in a tie finish against the Eagles. Through three games, Burrow had thrown 91 completions—the most completions by any rookie in NFL history in their first three starts.[xxxix]

Burrow had his third consecutive 300-yard game the following week and also his first win when the Bengals offense lit up the Jaguars for 33 points. Through four games, Burrow had six touchdowns and two picks while also running for a score.

In Burrow's second meeting against the Browns in Week 7, he again lit up the Browns defense, this time completing 35 of 47 passes for 406 yards and 3 touchdowns while also running for a touchdown. Burrow finished with a 112.5 rating but lost the game again to the Browns, this time 37-34.

Burrow threw a touchdown in 7 of his 10 starts that season. Unfortunately, his 10th game that year ended in tragedy. The 2-6-1 Bengals traveled to Washington to play the Football Team. Early in the third quarter of the game, Burrow was hit low and hard by two Washington defenders and immediately began clutching his knee. The injury looked extremely gruesome on television. Immediate thoughts were not only that Burrow's season was done, but also possibly his career as well. Burrow was carted off the field and replaced by backup Ryan Finley.

Shortly after the game, Burrow tweeted out, "See ya next year," knowing his season was finished. A couple of days later, it was announced that Burrow tore his ACL and MCL along with several other ligaments in his knee. Burrow, however, stayed positive, vowing to rehab and make it back for 2021.

"He was in great spirits," Bengals head coach Zac Taylor said. "On the bus, on the plane, you know, in the facility, he's responded as well as he possibly could and we've all noticed that."[xxxi]

It is important to stay positive in situations like that. When you get down, everyone else gets down and Burrow knew that. He was devastated over missing the rest of the season but needed to maintain a positive attitude for his team and push them forward. Because of that positive attitude, he helped Ryan Finley prepare for games. Thanks to Burrow's guidance, Finley would play the best football of his career at the end of the year, including a shocking road win in Pittsburgh.

"You can see how much Joe Burrow wants to win," wide receiver Tyler Boyd said. "I know how much he dedicates himself to the game."[xxxi]

Over the years, no one has said otherwise. A common theme has resonated around Joe Burrow. He is a leader. He is a team player. He is a competitor. He has a winning attitude that rubs off on everyone else. No one has said a bad thing about his work ethic and desire to better himself in the game.

Joe underwent surgery on his knee on December 2, 2020, and is recovering nicely. He began throwing in late February and is on target to be ready for the 2021 season. Given his remarkable dedication and determination, Joe Burrow's future in the NFL is nothing but bright.

Chapter 5: Personal Life

Some might describe the 24-year-old Joe Burrow as a little kid playing football. He is tough as nails on the pitch, but when it comes to his personal life, he has an unquenchable youthful exuberance that elevates the mood of everyone around him. It is what people love most about him.

Burrow is a "cartoon-geek" and is not shy about embracing that facet of his personality. He walks around sometimes with *SpongeBob Squarepants* clothes or some other iconic cartoon apparel. He still wakes up on Saturday morning to watch cartoons. He never was one for scary movies; although he loved *Star Wars* growing up, he stayed away from *Harry Potter* and *Lord of the Rings*. He has shown up to games wearing a suit with a Mr. Krabs picture on his jacket.

"I was scared of everything growing up," Burrow said. "I still don't like scary movies. I don't like haunted houses or anything like that. I couldn't watch *Harry Potter, House*, or *Lord of the Rings*. I was like, strictly a *SpongeBob*, Disney Channel, Nickelodeon kinda guy. I still am."[xxxii]

Burrow is occasionally seen wearing superhero t-shirts and even crunching on a caramel apple lollypop, which is one of his favorite daily snacks. Before the Heisman Trophy ceremony, he played video games—Pokemon, to be exact. When asked what one of his favorite hobbies was, Burrow replied, "Watching people at Walmart."[xxxv]

Burrow's child-like demeanor helps fuel his sense of humor. While he has always been more of the quiet type, he is good at making people laugh. In fact, Burrow has become an LSU icon not just for winning the national championship, but because he does some of the best Ed Orgeron impressions anyone has ever seen and has had his teammates on the floor laughing. He even did it at the Heisman Trophy ceremony.

It is one of the things his girlfriend Olivia Holzmacher adores about him. She says Joe always makes her laugh and smile. Olivia and Joe met at Ohio State in 2017 and have dated ever since, even while he transferred and she stayed back in Columbus to get her degree in 2019. She often posts pictures of them together, whether it be after games, at home, or even at the Heisman Trophy ceremony.

"I'm so proud of you," Holzmacher posted on her Instagram with a picture of her and Burrow at the Heisman Trophy ceremony in New York City. "The best weekend ever."[xxxiii]

Holzmacher has stayed by Burrow's side and wants to be at every one of his NFL games, but COVID-19 made it hard. So, when fans were not allowed into Paul Brown Stadium to watch the team's opening game against the Chargers, Holzmacher wanted to assure Joe that she was there. In the front row was a cardboard cutout so he could see her along with his parents.

By week 6, she was able to go to her first game when the Colts allowed fans to attend their game in a limited capacity. "Open the moon roof kinda day," she posted on her Instagram.[xxxiii]

In his free time, Burrow spends time learning how to play the guitar. He has so far mastered one song, Tom Petty's "Free Fallin'." He has played it maybe a thousand times, he says, but has not yet mastered any other legendary songs.

Burrow is also deeply rooted in his faith. He grew up going to church in Ohio and constantly thanks God for his success as a football player and getting him to the point he is at today.

Charity Work

In July 2020, Joe Burrow joined in support of the Athens Food Pantry and started the Joe Burrow Hunger Relief Fund, a program that gives food to low-income neighborhoods and families, particularly those in Ohio where he was born and raised.

"I'm so grateful for the outpouring of support from people across the country around the food insecurity issues faced by those in my region," Burrow said. "The initial funds that were raised have had an immediate impact for people throughout Athens County, and I am honored to lend my support and voice to this new initiative that will ensure that impact lasts long into the future."[xxxvi]

Burrow's relief fund became a success before he even became a professional and started the initiative. The week after his Heisman Trophy speech, Will Drabold's efforts raised over $650,000 for the Athens Food Pantry as a result of being motivated by Burrow's speech. The two now work together to feed families in need.

Thus far, the program has been a success. After Burrow's season ended against Washington, close to 1,300 fans donated $27,000 to the Human Relief Fund.

Burrow's charity will likely grow with time as he continues to build his legacy as a Cincinnati Bengal. He is currently entering his second year of a four-year, $36-million contract with a signing bonus of just under $24 million.[xxxvii]

Burrow currently has two endorsements, Nike and Bose. The number of endorsements will likely increase over the next few years as he settles into the NFL. Most rookie superstars only start off with one or two endorsements and then expand upon that, depending on their success.

Chapter 6: Legacy and Future

Joe Burrow's legacy in the NFL is still years away from being determined, but his legacy in college football has already been cemented. Statistics show that he is among the greatest college football quarterbacks to ever play the game. His 2019 season is also among the greatest years in collegiate history.

In 2019 alone, Burrow broke several all-time single-season records, including throwing 60 touchdown passes and combining for 65 overall touchdowns in one year. He also ties for third all-time and for most yards in a single season, throwing for 5,671 yards in one year. That number is an all-time SEC and LSU record.[xxxviii]

Burrow also stands third-all time for best completion percentage in a single season at 76.3 percent. Only Mac Jones from Alabama and Colt McCoy from Texas have achieved higher numbers, and just barely.[xxxviii]

Burrow's postseason success also includes records that may never be topped, at least in the short term. Burrow's eight combined touchdowns against Oklahoma in the Peach Bowl set an all-time FBS record; seven of those touchdowns came through the air, tying a bowl record. He also broke the all-time passing record for most yards in a championship game (463), most passing yards in the playoffs (956), and most yards of total offense in a championship game (521).[xxxviii]

Perhaps the record that Burrow is most proud of is his record as a starting quarterback. His .893 winning percentage and 25-3 record as a starter top all LSU quarterbacks in history who have had at least 10 starts. Burrow is also the first SEC quarterback to ever throw for 4,000 yards and 40 touchdowns in the same season. The fact that he threw for over 5,000 yards and 60 touchdowns makes that record nearly impossible to catch. He completely shattered the old record.[xxxviii]

Burrow's Ohio State days as a backup likely kept him from breaking many all-time records that other quarterbacks hold from a career standpoint. He ranks ninth all-time in completion percentage at 68.8. His 78 overall touchdowns rank 108th on the all-time list.[iii]

Burrow's unfortunate knee injury held him back from having one of the best rookie seasons, not only in Bengals history but also in NFL history. He tied Boomer Esiason for most 300-yard games as a Bengals rookie and finished just one shy of Andrew Luck for most all-time 300-yard games as a rookie. (All this while not even playing in 10 complete games!)[xxxix]

Because of his injury, it is hard to compare his overall yards and touchdowns to other NFL greats who played full years in their rookie season. However, his 65.3 completion percentage is among the best in NFL history for a rookie. By comparison, Peyton Manning had a 56.7 completion percentage his rookie year, Andrew Luck was 54.1, Tom Brady was 63.9 (his first full year as a starter), and Patrick Mahomes was 66 (his first full year as a starter).[xxix]

If Burrow had stayed healthy, he could have broken Andrew Luck's all-time record for most passing yards as a rookie, 4,374 yards. Burrow would have needed just under 1,700 in his final six-and-half starts to break that record, which is roughly 270 yards per game, an achievement definitely in reach. Justin Herbert came within 40 yards of breaking Luck's record in 2020.[xxix]

For Burrow, his driving force has always been to prove others wrong, those who did not believe in him or did not give him a shot. He was passed up for national All-Star games, such as the Under Armour High School All-America Game, in favor of other quarterbacks. He was told by Nebraska twice that he was not good enough to play for them. And while he thought he was the best quarterback at Ohio State, he was playing second fiddle to Dwayne Haskins, or so it appeared that way before he transferred.

"Mental notes," Burrow says. "I still remember quarterbacks that schools took ahead of me in high school."[iv]

"Not getting the starting job at Ohio State really messed with him mentally," his brother Dan said. "He thought he had won the job."[iv]

Burrow is not alone. Many quarterbacks have something that motivates or pushes them, and many times it is to prove others wrong. Do you think Tom Brady did not have a chip on his shoulder when he was selected in the sixth round of the 2001 NFL Draft? Or to prove to the league that he would win a Super Bowl without Bill Belichick as his coach? How about Kyler Murray, who was told repeatedly that he was too small to be an NFL quarterback? Or Adam Thielen, a superstar wide receiver who nobody wanted in college or the NFL and who had to work just to get a tryout?

All players have a common goal: to prove to themselves and others their capability. Burrow has already established himself as one of the greatest college football quarterbacks ever and has the potential to be one of the best the NFL has ever seen. One thing is for sure—you would be hard-pressed to find a more dedicated worker than Burrow, who has put his all into becoming the best quarterback and leader he can be. Perhaps no quote represents the kind of player Burrow can be in the NFL than that of his own head coach, Zac Taylor:

"You want your quarterback to be the hardest worker on the team and an extension of the coaching staff," Taylor said. He fits both those descriptions for us right now. He really breathes life into this offense, into this team."[xl]

But while Burrow has worked his butt off to get into the position he is now in, his leadership might be his best quality. Leadership goes a long way. There is not one person that has played with Burrow who has doubted his leadership abilities. His coaches, his teammates, and his family have all relished how good

Burrow was as the leader of the team, dating all the way back to high school.

"He's very confident, he's not arrogant," Taylor said. "I think the team believes in this guy right now, but again he's earned that in the way that he's gone about his work, the way he operates in the meetings, the way he communicates with his teammates on both sides of the ball," Taylor added. "He's filling into that leadership role as well as any young player can do right now."[xl]

Humility, leadership, respect, and work ethic are incredible qualities to have. To find that in a player is incredibly rare, and Joe Burrow has them all, along with an amazing talent that we can only surmise will take him a long way, not only in the NFL but in life.

Conclusion

The moment on that stage when he accepted the Heisman Trophy Award illustrated the kind of person Joe Burrow is. He is never one to think about himself, but always others. That includes football. While he always works hard to make himself better, he does it for the team. He thinks of ways to make the team better, and that includes doing what he can to chip in.

Burrow is as non-selfish an athlete as you will ever find in sports. He is the perfect role model for young athletes because who he is on the outside is also who he is on the inside. He truly plays for those kids in Ohio growing up in a poor environment to show that they can one day be like him if they put their mind and effort into it. He has illustrated that leadership is such an important quality to winning. By being a positive influence on others, you can achieve the most out of your team.

Burrow has been a winner his whole career—and against the odds. He went to a high school that was not very successful and then took them to the state championship. He went to LSU, a school that was struggling to find its identity since losing Nick Saban, and helped produce a national championship and one of the greatest offenses in college football history.

Now he has a new chapter to write with the Bengals, an underdog team that has also seen its share of struggles. It has been a long time since Cincinnati has produced a winning football team, but Burrow has the ability to help change that. It is too early to predict what the future will hold for this remarkably talented young man, but if he continues the positive mentality and leadership he has thus far exhibited, his legacy may well be one for the record books. Joe Burrow could truly become the face of the Bengals, the face of Ohio, and, perhaps one day, the face of the NFL itself.

Final Word/About the Author

I was born and raised in Norwalk, Connecticut. Growing up, I could often be found spending many nights watching basketball, soccer, and football matches with my father in the family living room. I love sports and everything that sports can embody. I believe that sports are one of the most genuine forms of competition, heart, and determination. I write my works to learn more about influential athletes in the hopes that from my writing, you the reader can walk away inspired to put in an equal if not greater amount of hard work and perseverance to pursue your goals. If you enjoyed *Joe Burrow: The Inspiring Story of One of Football's Rising Star Quarterbacks,* please leave a review! Also, you can read more of my works on *David Ortiz, Mike Trout, Bryce Harper, Jackie Robinson, Aaron Judge, Odell Beckham Jr., Bill Belichick, Serena Williams, Rafael Nadal, Roger Federer, Novak Djokovic, Richard Sherman, Andrew Luck, Rob Gronkowski, Brett Favre, Calvin Johnson,*

Drew Brees, J.J. Watt, Colin Kaepernick, Aaron Rodgers, Peyton Manning, Tom Brady, Russell Wilson, Odell Beckham Jr., Bill Belichick, Charles Barkley, Trae Young, Gregg Popovich, Pat Riley, John Wooden, Steve Kerr, Brad Stevens, Red Auerbach, Doc Rivers, Erik Spoelstra, Michael Jordan, LeBron James, Kyrie Irving, Klay Thompson, Stephen Curry, Kevin Durant, Russell Westbrook, Anthony Davis, Chris Paul, Blake Griffin, Kobe Bryant, Joakim Noah, Scottie Pippen, Carmelo Anthony, Kevin Love, Grant Hill, Tracy McGrady, Vince Carter, Patrick Ewing, Karl Malone, Tony Parker, Allen Iverson, Hakeem Olajuwon, Reggie Miller, Michael Carter-Williams, John Wall, James Harden, Tim Duncan, Steve Nash, Draymond Green, Kawhi Leonard, Dwyane Wade, Ray Allen, Pau Gasol, Dirk Nowitzki, Jimmy Butler, Paul Pierce, Manu Ginobili, Pete Maravich, Larry Bird, Kyle Lowry, Jason Kidd, David Robinson, LaMarcus Aldridge, Derrick Rose, Paul George, Kevin Garnett, Chris Paul, Marc Gasol, Yao Ming, Al Horford,

Amar'e Stoudemire, DeMar DeRozan, Isaiah Thomas, Kemba Walker, Chris Bosh, Andre Drummond, JJ Redick, DeMarcus Cousins, Wilt Chamberlain, Bradley Beal, Rudy Gobert, Aaron Gordon, Kristaps Porzingis, Nikola Vucevic, Andre Iguodala, Devin Booker, John Stockton, Jeremy Lin, Chris Paul, Pascal Siakam, Jayson Tatum, Gordon Hayward, Nikola Jokic, Bill Russell, Victor Oladipo, Luka Doncic, Ben Simmons, Shaquille O'Neal, Joel Embiid, Donovan Mitchell, Damian Lillard and *Giannis Antetokounmpo* in the Kindle Store. If you love football, check out my website at claytongeoffreys.com to join my exclusive list where I let you know about my latest books and give you lots of goodies.

Like what you read? Please leave a review!

I write because I love sharing the stories of influential athletes like Joe Burrow with fantastic readers like you. My readers inspire me to write more so please do not hesitate to let me know what you thought by leaving a review! If you love books on life, sports, or productivity, check out my website at claytongeoffreys.com to join my exclusive list where I let you know about my latest books. Aside from being the first to hear about my latest releases, you can also download a free copy of *33 Life Lessons: Success Principles, Career Advice & Habits of Successful People*. See you there!

Clayton

References

[i] King, Peter. "'Thank God for Joe Burrow': A Heisman Trophy Speech That Raised Nearly Half a Million in Charity. *NBC Sports.* 23 Dec 2019. Web.

[ii] "Joe Burrow Speech: 2019 Heisman Trophy Presentation." *YouTube.* 2019. Media.

[iii] "Joe Burrow College Stats." Sports-Reference." Nd. Web.

[iv] Dellenger, Ross. "Joe Burrow's Remarkable Rise Has Been Beyond Even His Wildest Dreams." *Sports Illustrated.* 26 Nov 2019. Web.

[v] Bender, Bill. "Get to Know Joe Burrow, from Ohio State's Mr. Football, Transfer to LSU & a Legendary Heisman Season." *Sporting News.* 23 Apr 2020. Web.

[vi] Shapiro, Michael. "Ed Orgeron: LSU 'So Grateful' for Joe Burrow After National Championship Victory." *Sports Illustrated.* 14 Jan 2020. Web.

[vii] Sigler, John. "Joe Burrow Reflects on Meeting Drew Brees, 'My Idol.'" *USA Today.* 25 Feb 2020. Web.

[viii] Chornobroff, Shaun. "Joe Burrow was Always Destined for Stardom." *The Wrightway Sports Network.* 2 Feb 2020. Web.

[ix] Schmidt, Patrick. "Pride of the Plains: Hometown Hero Joe Burrow." *Fansided.com.* Nd. Web.

[x] Smalley, Jerod. "Joe Burrow's Family Embraces Long Road from Athens, to OSU, to LSU." *NBC4i.com.* 11 Dec 2019. Web.

[xi] Wiseman, Adam. "Burrow Was Also a Basketball Standout." *The Athens Messenger.* 27 Nov 2019. Web.

[xii] Mickles, Sheldon. "Ultimate Competitor: Joe Burrow's Work Ethic Storied High School Career Could Bode Well for LSU." *The Advocate.* 1 Jun 2018. Web.

[xiii] "Joe Burrow: Athens High School." *MaxPreps.* Nd. Web.

[xiv] Dyer, Mike. "From Bulldog to Tiger: Joe Burrow is the Pride of Athens County." *WCPO.com.* 27 Jan 2020. Web.

[xv] "Joe Burrow Still Thankful Tom Herman Believed in Him When Few Did: 'I Owe a Lot to Coach Herman.'" *Saturday Down South.* Nd. Web.

[xvi] Peterson, Randy. "Heisman Trophy Front-Runner Burrow Will Forever Be Linked to Ames and That House on McKinley Drive." *The Des Moines Register*. 13 Dec 2019. Web.

[xvii] Al-Khateeb, Zac. "Where Did Joe Burrow Transfer From? Why the Heisman Winner Left Ohio State for LSU" *Sporting News*. 23 Apr 2020. Web.

[xviii] "Dwayne Haskins College Stats." *Sports-Reference*. Nd. Web.

[xix] "How Dwayne Haskins Beat Joe Burrow Out for the Starting Position at Ohio State." *NBC Sports*. 21 Jan 2020. Web.

[xx] Dellenger, Ross. "How Ed Orgeron and LSU Landed Game-Changer QB Transfer Joe Burrow." *Sports Illustrated*. 29 May 2018. Web.

[xxi] O'Gara, Connor. "The One That Got Away? Urban Meyer, Ohio State Players on Why LSU Should Be Excited About Joe Burrow." *Saturday Down South*. 2018. Web.

[xxii] "No. 11 LSU Knocks Off No. 7 UCF 40-32 in Fiesta Bowl." *ESPN.com*. 1 Jan 2019. Web.

[xxiii] "Burrow's 3 TDs Lift No. 5 LSU over No. 7 Florida." *ESPN.com*. 13 Oct 2019. Web.

[xxiv] "Joe Burrow Leads No. 3 LSU Past No. 2 Alabama in 46-41 Thriller." *ESPN.com*. 9 Nov 2019. Web.

[xxv] "2019 Heisman Trophy Voting." *Sports-Reference*. Nd. Web.

[xxvi] "Burrow Throws 7 TDs, NO. 1 LSU Routs No. 4 Oklahoma 63-28." *ESPN.com*. 28 Dec 2019. Web.

[xxvii] "Burrow, LSU Cap Heisman Season, Beat Clemson 42-25 for Title." *ESPN.com*. 14 Jan 2020. Web.

[xxviii] Embody, Billy. "Everything Joe Burrow Said After Cincinnati Bengals Drafted Him." *247Sports.com*. 27 Apr 2020. Web.

[xxix] "Joe Burrow NFL Stats." *Pro-Football Reference*. Nd. Web.

[xxx] "Burrow Runs for TD But Chargers Rally 16-13 Over Bengals." *ESPN.com*. 13 Sep 2020. Web.

[xxxi] Schefter, Adam. "Torn ACL, MCL, Plus More Knee Damage for Cincinnati Bengals QB Joe Burrow, Sources Say." *ESPN.com*. 23 Nov 2020. Web.

[xxxii] Gaydos, Ryan. "Joe Burrow Reveals Why He Stuck with Cartoons Instead of Famous Flicks." *Fox News*. 12 Nov 2020. Web.

[xxxiii] Hendricks, Jaclyn. "Who is Bengals Quarterback Joe Burrow's Girlfriend? Meet Olivia Holzmacher." *Page Six*. 1 Nov 2020. Web.

xxxiv Mickles, Sheldon. "Watch Joe Burrow Q&A: How Many Sports Illustrated Covers Has LSU's QB Signed? 'Couldn't Even Tell You.'" *SI.com.* 2 Dec 2019. Web.

xxxv Thamel, Pete. "5 Things Bengals Fans Should Know About Joe Burrow." *Yahoo Sports.* 23 Apr 2020. Web.

xxxvi Werner, Barry. "Joe Burrow Hunger Relief Fund Becomes a Reality." *The USA Today.* 9 Jul 2020. Web.

xxxvii Haislop, Todd. "Joe Burrow Contract Breakdown: How Much Money Does Joe Burrow Make as a Rookie?" *Sporting News.* 17 Sep 2020. Web.

xxxviii Bender, Bill. "Nine Absurd Records Joe Burrow Set in LSU's College Football Playoff Championship Season." *Sporting News.* 14 Jan 2020. Web.

xxxix Bender, Bill. "Burrow's Rookie of The Year Season Marching To NFL And Bengals Record Books." *Bengals.com.* 26 Oct 2020. Web.

xl Nocco, Joseph. "Bengals Coach Shares Remarkable Quote About Joe Burrow and the Bengals Offense." *Clutch Points.* 25 Aug 2020. Web.

Made in the USA
Middletown, DE
31 January 2023

23630407R00068